PA
GAMES

PARTY GAMES

Jessica Davies

PIATKUS

© 1988 Jessica Davies

First published in 1988 by
Judy Piatkus (Publishers) Limited,
5 Windmill Street, London W1P 1HF

British Library Cataloguing in Publication Data

Davies, Jessica
  Party games.
  1. Party games. Collections
  I. Title
  793.2

  ISBN 0–86188–783–2
  ISBN 0–86188–788–3 Pbk

Illustrated by Teri Gower
Designed by Sue Ryall

Photoset in 11/13pt Compugraphic Futura Book by
Action Typesetting Ltd, Gloucester
Printed and bound in Great Britain by
Billing and Sons, Limited, Worcester

TO MUM AND DAD
WITH LOVE

Thank you to all those people — friends and family — who not only told me of games I did not know, but who also spent time explaining and playing them with me.

Contents

Introduction

'The true object of all human life is play'
G.K. Chesterton

Parlour games are back in vogue. Not since Victorian times have they been so popular. Perhaps it's something to do with the fact that we're all rather austere these days, and the liberating frivolity of a good old-fashioned game offers a welcome contrast to the serious business of daily life. Whatever it is, people seem to have cottoned on to the fact that standing in a crowded room, drink in hand and shouting at each other is a pretty pointless activity, and that cavorting round the house in blindfolds and the like is, frankly, much more fun.

Nowhere are games more essential than at that annual ordeal: The Family Christmas Party. Cast your mind back to the last one, and the grossly incompatible company that was present. You'll have had the Oldies: Batty Great Aunt Beatrix: and Uncle Fred from Australia, dispatched to England for the season by his shrewd children. Then there will have been an assortment of unloved misfits: a truculent teenager or two, that difficult second cousin (your turn this year), the Japanese gentleman from Head Office, and so on.

There'll have been arguments over the television (Great Aunt B and 'The Sound of Music' versus Snooker or 'Top of the Pops') and arguments over whose turn it was to lend a sympathetic ear to Uncle Fred's tales of the Bush, his bungalow and his dear dead wife. And that's just for starters.

1

The point is that Nature never intended these people to enjoy each other's company, and left to their own devices they can turn most festive occasions into pretty glum affairs.

With a few games, however, you can defy even Mother Nature. The trick is to be well prepared, to plan in advance the games you intend to play, and to be sure you have the appropriate props. You can also warn people before they arrive that you intend to play some games — they're far less likely to balk at the suggestion if they've been given time to work up a little enthusiasm for the idea.

Games will never just 'happen', and if you think you can rely on inspiration or the resources of your guests, you will find yourself looking pretty foolish. A little imagination is essential. There is no point, for instance, in brightly suggesting *Musical Bumps* or *Murder on all Fours* to the old and the fragile; nor is it reasonable to expect the chronically shy to relish the prospect of an entire evening of acting games. You do, after all, want people to have a good time.

Careful preparation does not preclude a certain flexibility. If your guests decide they want to play *The Game* ten times over, let them. Don't bulldoze them through the twenty games you've listed just for the sake of it. Most good parties will only get through five or six.

An enthusiastic Master of Ceremonies — one of those loud, red-faced buffoons (usually to be found in the vicinity of the bar) — is an invaluable aide. He will cajole the unadventurous into playing, ensure that house rules prevail, and see that cheating is done only in moderation.

Prizes are important too. The chances are that you will already have spent a fortune on food and drinks, so the last thing you want to do is splash out on extravagant gifts. Tokens are really all that's required and here are some suggestions:

★ A *Beano* annual.
★ A bag of Maltesers.
★ A wind-up duck for the bath.

★ Chocolate money.
★ Pink plastic sunglasses.
★ A rubber tarantula.
★ Mini *Mars* Bars.
★ A sugar mouse.
★ This book.
★ A silly hat.
★ A bag of balloons.
★ A pack of playing cards.
★ A stick-on moustache.
★ A miniature bottle of brandy or whisky.

It's always a good idea to have more prizes than you think you're going to need. It can be embarrassing to run out in the middle of the party — you'd be amazed how disappointed people can be!

Forfeits are also a must, and these could include:

★ Forming a line, and spanking your victim as he crawls between your legs.
★ Wearing something ridiculous for the rest of the evening — for a man this could be a pink hair bow; for a woman it could be a stick-on moustache.
★ Eating a raw egg.
★ Standing on a chair and singing the National Anthem.
★ Running into the nearest bedroom and putting on the first piece of clothing in sight.
★ Streaking round the garden in a pair of wellies.
★ Speaking Swahili for the rest of the evening.
★ Going out, latching on to a passer-by and bringing him or her back to the party.
★ Doing a head/handstand in the middle of the room.
★ Wearing a dunce's hat.

Throughout the text I have generally referred to players as 'he'. This goes against the grain, but I found using both 'he' and 'she' too cumbersome — some of the games are hard enough to explain without additional complications. I hope anyone who is irritated by this will forgive me!

There are 101 games in this book. Some of them are common currency (*Charades, The Game*, etc), and others are known only to a select few (*Russian Omelette, The Wind and the Leaves*). They represent a cross-section of what people are playing at parties today. Many would doubtless make the Victorians' hair stand on end, but they will at least ensure that next time you throw a party, *all* of your guests will go away saying they've had the time of their lives.

PARTY
GAMES

1
GAMES
for getting going

Parties are like pigs. You can't push them, but you can lead them. And if you propose playing party games, you'll have to seize the initiative the minute your guests walk through the door. Left to their own devices with the punch and the prawn vol-au-vents, they may either launch into wearisome conversations about house prices and hernias, or (and this is worse) loiter mutely self-conscious around the peanut bowl, wishing they could go home.

Parlour games can put a stop to any of this. Once you've played one or two, you'll find that even complete strangers, and people who have precious little in common, will be laughing together as if they've been best buddies for years.

It goes without saying that it would be both cruel and pointless to start the proceedings with anything as *louche* as *Russian Omelette* or *The Dream Game.* You don't want to frighten people away. No, what you need at this stage is a gently persuasive introduction and follow-up to the pleasures of the parlour game. This will allow your guests to meet, drink and let their hair down before the serious playing begins . . .

FINDING YOUR PARTNER

Props: A pencil, paper and pins

Preparation: Draw up a list of famous partnerships and decide how you plan to pair off your guests

If you think this is some sort of liberal exercise in marriage-broking, or the naughty prelude to an orgy, you're in for a disappointment. *Finding Your Partner* is mild stuff, despite the fact that some people call it *Lovers*.

Before your guests arrive, draw up a list of famous partnerships — Laurel and Hardy, Samson and Delilah, Minnie and Mickey Mouse, Popeye and Olive, JR and Sue Ellen, you know the sort of thing. You then decide who you will pair off with whom. Don't be tempted into matchmaking — your friends will only blame you when it goes sour.

As they walk through the door, you pin a name on each of your guests' backs. Their task is to discover who they are, and then to track down their partner. The game continues until everyone has arrived and found their other half.

Finding out who you are is achieved by mingling and asking questions along the lines of 'Am I alive/dead/female/Tanzanian?' and so forth. Players may only ask three questions of another player, and they must then move on; this rule prevents your statutory Lonely and Long-Winded Guest from latching on to your statutory Good Listener. The only answer that may be given to any of the questions is 'Yes' or 'No'.

Once all the players have arrived, have discovered who they are, and are standing bashfully with their new-found friends, you can set them off on a few innocuous warm-up games. These could include *Kim's Game, Chopsticks, Hidden Objects, Straws, Famous Faces, Baby Faces* and *The Back-to-Back-Race*. Each partnership scores points for every game, and the overall winners win a prize.

A final word. This is not a wise choice of game if you have odd numbers or if you have no idea how many are turning up. It's always the Deeply Sensitive Poet who manages to end up partnerless, and who, with dignity ruffled, will flee from the party in tears.

WHO AM I?

Props: A pencil, paper and pins

Preparation: Draw up a list of famous people

A variation on *Finding Your Partner*, with the advantage that it can be played with odd numbers.

This time you must think up a list of famous individuals — Joan of Arc, Henry VIII, Cleopatra and Winnie the Pooh, for instance. Once more, each player has a piece of paper bearing one of the names pinned to his back as he arrives. And once more, whether he likes it or not, he must circulate and ask questions to find out who he is.

It's likely that some of your guests will work out who they are long before the others do — especially if there are late arrivals. This does not matter, as the game will have broken the ice, and people will happily continue talking until the last player has discovered his identity.

Anybody who is caught talking about jobs, mortgages or other such humdrum affairs should be marked down for a practical joke later in the evening (see Chapter 7).

ANIMAL FAMILIES

Props: None

Preparation: Think up a list of obscure animals and practise crawling around on all fours and grunting

Another ice-breaker. This is quite a silly game, and some of your more square friends may refuse to cooperate. If nothing else, it will show you who not to invite next time round, and who should be the butt of a joke later on in the evening (again see Chapter 7).

As with *Finding Your Partner* and *Who Am I?*, the object of the game is to dispense with inhibitions and get the party going.

Your preparation involves thinking up a list of animal families — daddy gerbil, mummy gerbil, and baby gerbil, for instance. You secretly tell each of your guests which member of which animal family he is to be, and once everybody is present, you issue the following instruction:

'Down on your knees!'

Down they all go, and begin crawling around the room making the noise appropriate to their species. (What gerbils do, I cannot say.)

The object, amid the cacophony, is for each person to find the rest of his or her animal family, and to pile on to a chair (daddy at the bottom, baby on top, with mummy sandwiched somewhere in the middle). This is generally more uncomfortable than exciting.

The first completed family wins, and should be given a prize.

Species to keep them guessing could include anteater, rhinoceros, pig, bear, llama, giraffe and laughing hyena!

MISSIONS

Props: None

Preparation: Decide on a mission for each of your guests — this *could* take time!

The only game in the book which can be played from the beginning of the party right through to the end of the evening, while playing other games at the same time.

Everybody is given a mission. Here are some examples of what these might be:

★ Express violent political opinions — either far left or right wing will do.
★ Wink whenever a member of the opposite sex looks at you.
★ Be consistently cheeky/charming to whoever is sitting next to you.
★ Burst into hysterical fits of giggles whenever the clock strikes the hour.
★ Talk endlessly about your job/mother/heart condition.
★ Pretend you know lots of famous people and keep dropping their names into the conversation.

The idea is to carry out your mission during the course of the entire evening — and to do so subtly. If, therefore, your detail is to be insulting, you should refrain from comments like: 'Boy does your breath smell,' or 'You're too old/fat for mini skirts.' They're a give-away. Something a little more sly, along the lines of 'There's this friend of mine with a real halitosis problem ' will work better.

When the party winds up, everyone should have dropped enough clues for everyone else to guess their mission. If it's generally agreed that a player hasn't, he should be made to pay a forfeit.

YES AND NO

Props: Five coins or matches per player

Preparation: None

A game which will force even the most churlish of guests to make some sort of conversation. The idea is to hang on to your matches/coins while trying to make other players give up theirs. This could follow on after *Finding Your Partner*.

Players are given five coins each (or five matches if you're hard up), and then divided into pairs. Each player engages his partner in conversation, asking him questions with the aim of tricking him into using either 'Yes' or 'No' in his answer. Whoever succeeds in doing this, gives a coin or match to his partner.

The players then split up, mingle, form new partnerships and start new conversations. The first player to get rid of his five coins wins.

KIM'S GAME

Props: A pencil and paper for each player/pair of players, a tray, a cloth and a collection of small objects

Preparation: Before the party begins, you should set out twenty or so small objects on a tray: a thimble, a stamp, a hairpin, a grape, a feather, a false tooth — whatever takes your fancy — and cover the lot with a cloth

Everyone gathers round the tray, the cloth is whipped off, and players have 30 seconds in which to memorise the objects. When the cloth is replaced they are given two or three minutes to draw up a list of the items they can remember. Players get a point for each object correctly remembered, and the highest score wins.

Other objects could include a match, a pencil sharpener, a ring, a button, a paper clip, a walnut, a cork and a grain of rice.

HIDDEN OBJECTS

Props: A pencil and paper for each player/pair of players and a selection of objects

Preparation: Some forethought and about ten minutes to hide the objects about the house

This game will test players' powers of observation, and should therefore be played at the beginning of the evening before people begin seeing double, treble and pink elephants.

By way of preparation, various objects are placed around the house. They must all be at least partially visible in an obviously incorrect place, but in no way conspicuous. You could stick a stamp in the corner of a busy picture, lie a knitting needle along the edge of a picture frame, or stick a piece of spaghetti in a dried flower arrangment, for example.

The players are given a list of all the hidden objects and the run of the house. Whenever they spot one of the objects, they must secretly make a note of its whereabouts and casually pretend they have seen nothing. The first player to find all the objects wins.

Your more excitable friends may spoil matters by whooping with delight, or whispering loudly and pointing whenever they discover one of the objects. Such people should be made to pay a forfeit.

FAMOUS FACES

Props: Pictures of celebrities — about twenty — cut from magazines and newspapers, a pencil and paper per player and some *blue-tac*

Preparation: Be sure you know who all the famous faces are!

If you have one of those parties where nobody knows anybody, or where you seem to have gathered under your roof an uncommon number of social idiots, this is the game for you. People can talk to each other if they want. But if they don't, neither you nor they will be embarrassed.

Having chosen and cut out your twenty pictures, you should number them and stick them to the wall.

As people arrive, present them with their drink, paper and pencil, and send them over to the wall of pictures. Their task is to identify and name the faces.

Sociable types will cheat from the outset, peering over shoulders in a jocular fashion and comparing answers. The timid and the taciturn will take it all very seriously, burying their noses in their pieces of paper and thus avoiding talking to anyone. Everyone, in short, will be happy.

After half an hour or so you should stop the game, read out the answers, give a point for each correct guess and a prize to whoever has the highest score.

BABY FACES

Props: A picture of everyone as a baby, blu-tac, paper and pencils

Preparation: Warn your guests that each must come armed with a picture of himself when small

There is nothing some people enjoy more than to show other people pictures of themselves as a baby (though of course they will deny this). 'Wasn't I a little fatty?' they'll say, pointing fondly at their portly 2½ year old self and pausing expectantly for a sugary response. Such narcissists will love this game.

Everybody must come to the party bearing a photo of himself as a baby. The pictures are labelled with a number, and stuck up on the wall. Armed with a pencil and paper, each player tries to guess which baby is which of the other players.

All may not be as it seems. I have found that the prettiest babies grow into the ugliest adults, and vice versa. Likewise, the babies kitted out in the frilliest frocks are invariably male. You can be sure of only one thing: that anyone who arrives photo-less was very plain when small.

CHOPSTICKS

Props: Chopsticks, two plates and a bag of frozen peas

Preparation: Put some peas in the freezer and leave them there for at least six hours; go on holiday to China

A very simple game which can be played in pairs after, say, *Finding Your Partner*, Players have to transfer peas from one plate to another, using chopsticks. There is a time limit of 30 seconds in which to perform this uncommonly difficult feat and whoever shifts the greatest number of peas in this time is the winner.

Adept chopstick-handlers can be handicapped by playing blindfolded or with their left hand.

STRAWS

Props: Drinking straws, two plates and a bag of frozen peas

Preparation: As for *Chopsticks*, but without the China bit

A variation of *Chopsticks* in which players are timed as they suck, one at a time, a given number of peas up on the end of a straw and transfer them from one plate to another. The player who shifts the peas in the shortest time wins.

A more sophisticated version of the game involves pushing the straw up your nostril, sniffing to pick up the pea from the first plate and running once round the room before depositing it on the second plate. No hands allowed of course.

SNIFF

Props: Ten pegs, ten envelopes, ten scented objects and a clothes line

Preparation: Take lots of vitamin C

This game is for those whose olfactory organs are in perfect working order, and should not be attempted by anyone with a head cold. It's another suitable follow-up to *Finding Your Partner* as you can play it in pairs.

Put into each envelope something which has its own distinctive smell. Some orange peel, a clove of garlic, a sprig of mint, a lump of parmesan cheese would all be suitable. Then prick a hole in the envelope and peg it to the clothes line.

The players are led in, one by one, blindfolded. They must smell each bag (no hands allowed) and guess the contents. Whoever makes the most correct guesses is the winner.

TASTE

Props: Cups, potable liquids and a blindfold

Preparation: Practise by going on a pub crawl

A variation on *Sniff*. This time it is your palate that's put to work. Again, some preparation is necessary. You need about ten cups or glasses set out on a table and filled with a variety of drinkable liquids – whisky, brandy, wine, milk, cold coffee, iced tea, crème de menthe, cold stock, etc.

The players are led in, one by one, blindfolded. They must take a sip of each cup and then identify the contents. The winner is whoever makes the most correct guesses.

BACK-TO-BACK RACE

Props: None

Preparation: Clear your biggest room of valuables

A game to be played after *Finding Your Partner*, as you compete in pairs.

Everybody lines up at the end of the room, back-to-back with their partner, arms linked at the elbows. At the word 'Go!' the pairs race to the far end of the room, and back again. The first linked pair to return to base wins.

A small word of warning. Be sensible about who is attached to whom. Although it is obviously amusing to pair-up opposites — the very tall with the very short, for instance — your octogenarian grandmother may object to being dragged up and down the drawing room by a competitive 15-year-old.

Useful variations on this game include those old favourites *The Three-Legged Race*, where players race up and down the room with one leg tied to one of their partner's legs, *The Piggy-Back Race*, where large players have to carry their little (with luck) partners, and *The Wheelbarrow Race*. Watch out for slipped discs and dicky hearts.

2
GAMES
for guests
who hate games

Some people have a real aversion to games, and will be quite determined in their resistance to any jamboree you might suggest. Maybe someone sat on them in a game of *Musical Bumps* when they were small. Or maybe they're simply frightened of making fools of themselves. You just can't tell. And *they* won't.

They are parlour game saboteurs, professional party poopers, and a nuisance. But what's worse is that their lack of enthusiasm can spread like an epidemic. You won't ask them back to this sort of party — keep them on the list for dinners and drinks. However, for the time being you're stuck with them.

Fortunately, if you are resourceful there is no reason why non-players should stop the rest of you from having a ball. The games in this chapter should help you survive that dreadful moment when your Difficult Guest stamps his foot, crosses his arms and stubbornly declares that he is *not joining in*.

SARDINES

Props: None

Preparation: Life

The mildly erotic associations of a round of *Sardines* will usually persuade your uncooperative guest (and there'll always be one) that games aren't all that bad. And if that doesn't work, don't worry — simply pack the person off as your first Sardine. He'll be glad to get away from the rest of you, and you'll be glad to be rid of his complaining countenance.

Off he goes to find a hiding place somewhere in the house. Having given him plenty of time to do this, the rest of you turn out the lights (it's much better in the dark) and creep off into the shadows to find the Sardine's lair.

If you discover the Sardine, and other players are nearby, you should feign nonchalance until they are out of sight. As soon as the coast's clear, you join the Sardine in the airing cupboard, under the bed, up the chimney or wherever, and wait with him until one by one all the other players find you. Some delightfully titillating tête-a-têtes can ensue, but they rarely last for long.

There are no winners or losers in a game of *Sardines* — just a few bruised ribs, cricked necks and (occasionally) the odd lipstick-smeared collar and guilty conscience. The first or last to arrive on the scene can be the next Sardine.

THE DRAWING GAME

Props: Several sheets of paper, pencils, two teams and three rooms

Preparation: Enrol in a course of evening classes at your local art school

Send your Difficult Guest into one of the rooms — say, the kitchen — and tell him he must draw up a list of famous people, book titles, films, plays and so on. A dozen names and titles should be about right. This is an excellent task for the DG; it will make him feel both superior and important, and he is likely to produce a fiendish list, which is exactly what you want.

While he's thus occupied, the rest of you divide yourselves into two teams, and two rooms.

With his list completed, the DG calls out 'I'M READY!' or whatever, and one member of each team races out to the kitchen to discover the first name or title on the list.

The pair then dash back to their respective teams and communicate this name/title to their team mates — by means of drawing. As soon as some bright spark guesses the name correctly, it becomes his turn to discover the next name or title on the list and draw it for his team. The game continues until one team has successfully worked its way through the list.

If you get Gorbachev you're lucky: you simply draw a face with a squashed strawberry on its forehead — there aren't many people around who look like that. If you get a member of the royal family, you draw a crown and you're half way there. The Bible's quite straightforward too (a book and a cross), and so is *A Tale of Two Cities* (well, relatively). But how do you draw *Madame Bovary*, *Pride and Prejudice* or Elgar's *Enigma Variations*?

You're not supposed to write out any words, or speak

when it is your turn to draw. But a great many people do. And the sorry fact is that the team that wins (i.e. draws its way through the list first) is generally the team that has cheated the most. A referee in each room might help.

MUSICAL CUSHIONS

Props: Cushions (one fewer than there are players) and music

Preparation: Make sure you have plenty of cushions and a functioning record-player, piano or similar

Another exceedingly childish game which is recommended only for the fit and the fearless. Not easy if you're wearing a mini-skirt or if you suffer from either gout or palpitations.

Again, if you have a Difficult Guest in your midst, he or she is banished to the record player or the piano. The rest of you encircle a double row of cushions – make sure there are fewer cushions than there are players.

When the music strikes up, you all dance/hop/skip round the cushions. When the music stops you must try to plant your bottom in the nearest cushion – before anybody else does. the player who is left cushion-less drops out of the game.

Another cushion is now removed, so that you are again one short. When the music starts once more, the whole mad process is repeated, until only one player remains. The winner is usually the player blessed with the largest derrière, and he should be given a prize.

MUSICAL STATUES

Props: Music

Preparation: As for *Musical Cushions*, minus the cushions

A handy variation on *Musical Cushions*, for guests who are a little less robust.

The principle is exactly the same, except that this time when the music stops, players have to freeze in whatever position they find themselves in. The person who is controlling the music then walks around the room and picks out whoever sways, twitches or otherwise loses control.

Once several players have been eliminated, it's amusing for the losers to wander among the surviving players, pulling faces and trying to make them giggle.

The game continues until one self-controlled individual outlasts the others.

PASS THE ORANGE

Props: Two oranges

Preparation: Give some thought to dividing the teams fairly

Even the most obstructive of guests will play this game. It involves some rather racy body contact and will therefore always appeal.

You need two oranges and two teams (although you may have more teams and oranges if you wish.) The two teams line up in parallel, and at the word 'Go!' the person at the head of each team wedges an orange under his chin (difficult if it's of the receding variety) and turns to the next person down the line. Some interesting acrobatics now ensue, as 'A' endeavours to pass the orange from under his chin to 'B', who must receive it under his chin. NO HANDS are allowed, and if the orange drops, whoever is responsible must get down on all fours, and pick it up between chest and chin.

Each team passes its orange from player to player in this fashion, and the team that wins is, of course, the team that gets its orange to the end of the line first.

(If you want to be certain of winning, make sure all the chinless wonders are in the other team.)

PASS THE BOTTLE

Props: Two (empty) bottles

Preparation: Practise limbo-dancing

An x-rated version of *Pass The Orange*, as the bottle is clasped between players' knees and passed on by means of some rather dubious manoeuvres.

Again, you need two teams. No hands are allowed, and if anyone lets their bottle slip, they must crouch down and pick it up again with their knees. The winning team is the one that passes its bottle to the end of the line first.

FEET COMPETITION

Props: A screen of some sort — an old sheet or blanket, for instance

Preparation: None... save, perhaps, a visit to the chiropodist!

Anyone who is refusing to enter into the spirit of things can be given the very dull job of holding the screen in place. All the women now remove their shoes, tights, stockings, pop socks (well, it takes all sorts...) and stand in a row behind the screen, with only their ankles and feet showing beneath it.

One by one, each man walks down the line of feet and attempts to identify which pair belongs to whom. Husbands invariably fail to identify their own wives' trotters — especially if these are swollen-ankled and bulging with bunions. The scope for amusement is therefore infinite.

You can, alternatively, turn this game into a sort of beauty contest, and give a prize to whoever has the finest pair of ankles. My grandfather was once the recipient of such a prize when, at a village fête, he crept behind the screen with all the local belles. He did have *lovely* legs.

KNEES UP

Props: A blindfold for each female player

A variation on the *Feet Competition*, but no screen is needed. This time it's the men who have to go on parade, having first removed their trousers and exposed their knees. Among the prudish, rolling up trouser legs will suffice.

The women are sent out of the room while the men take off their trousers and line up ready for inspection. When they are ready, the women return — blindfolded. One by one, they must feel their way down the line of naked knees and try to guess which pair belongs to whom.

Once more, wives and girlfriends are usually quite unable to correctly identify their partners' knees.

If you have any Difficult Guests or killjoys in your midst, they will either run away or beg for another round — in either case, your problem is neatly solved.

IDENTITY PARADE

Props: A large sheet with a small hole in it, pencils and paper

Another relation of the *Feet Competition*.

Half of the players — all the men or all the women is easiest — assemble behind a large sheet which is held in place by anybody who thinks they are too mature/respectable/ serious-minded to indulge in such frivolity.

Each of the hidden players takes it in turn to poke his or her nose through the hole in the sheet. The players on the other side of the sheet each have a numbered list, and they must try and put a name to each nose — this can be an exceedingly difficult task, especially if some of the players have just met for the first time.

Once each nose has been noted and named, the players change places. Whoever comes up with the highest number of correct guesses is, naturally, the winner.

3
GAMES
for guests with
homicidal tendencies

Murdering each other is one of the most congenial ways of spending an evening. This unwholesome truth is borne out by the popularity of murder games, for which otherwise gentle, law-abiding individuals appear to have a passion.

It's largely to do with the dark, of course. Many of these games are played with lights off, and pulses race with the prospect of forbidden liaisons formed and kisses snatched when no-one else can see.

And then there's the danger too. A round of *Murder in the Dark* can reduce most parties to screaming hysteria. And even *Wink Murder* and *The Hangman* can give you a frisson if they are played in the right, sinister spirit. It therefore follows that if you have a houseful of nervous types, you might give this chapter a miss.

On the other hand, if your friends are made of more hardy stuff and you embark upon these games, you are likely to stick with them for the rest of the evening. They're addictive. So be sure that you know what you are letting yourself in for.

MURDER IN THE DARK

Props: A pack of playing cards

Preparation: None, although a stiff drink wouldn't go amiss

The best and most popular of the murdering games, this should really be played in a large country house with a resident ghost. Failing that, most other dark places will do.

Each player draws a card. Whoever draws the Jack of Hearts is the Detective (bad luck — you miss out on all the excitement); whoever draws the Ace of Spades is the Murderer. The latter conceals his identity, but the former declares himself and turns off all the lights. This is where the fun begins.

You all disappear into the shadows, hearts filled with terror, bumping into each other and most other things too (fragile family heirlooms should be locked away in the attic). The Murderer wanders among you, waiting for a moment when he is alone with his Victim, and then he strikes.

There are many ways of doing this. Clearly, whispering 'You're dead!' in somebody's ear is a little pathetic, as is pinching their bottom (sadly a favourite of older male Murderers.) Good Murderers wrap their fingers around their Victim's neck. Good Victims count to five before issuing a blood-curdling scream and falling prostrate on the floor.

Your Detective, who has been killing time in the drinks cupboard, now leaps into authoritative action, switching the lights back on and ordering you all to assemble — in the library, if you are lucky enough to have one. He then grills everyone (excepting the corpse) with questions running along these lines:

'Where were you when Uncle Claude screamed?'
'Were you in the same room as Uncle Claude when he was murdered?'

'Did you see anyone following Uncle Claude into the room?'

Everybody must answer truthfully, except for the Murderer who may spin whatever yarn he likes. From your answers, the Detective must choose his suspect and accuse. If he gets it wrong he must submit to a forfeit: if he gets it right he wins a prize.

WINK MURDER

Props: A pack of playing cards

Preparation: None

This is a genteel variation on the theme of *Murder in the Dark*. It's an excellent alternative when you have elderly people in your midst who might cause themselves — or the house — untold damage if left to wander about in the dark.

You all sit round a table and draw a card — whoever draws the Ace of Spades is Murderer. Everybody keeps their card concealed, and stares intently into everybody else's eyes. When the Murderer is satisfied that he is holding somebody's attention, and that nobody else is looking, he winks. The unfortunate Victim counts to five then gasps and drops his head on the table.

Provided that nobody intercepts the wink, the Murderer continues to bump people off until — if he is successful — there are no Victims left to wink at.

VAMPIRE

Props: A pack of cards and a blindfold per player (optional)

Preparation: Another case for a stiff drink

This game may sound a touch absurd, but it is surprisingly scary.

One of you is secretly designated the Vampire by drawing the Ace of Spades from a pack of cards.

Off go the lights, and everybody — including the Vampire — shuts their eyes (blindfolding is even better) and wanders round the room. The Vampire strikes by throttling anyone he bumps into (or, if you want to be risqué, by biting them on the neck.)

Once you have been throttled — or bitten — then you too become a Vampire and start killing Victims of your own.

If that's all there was to this game, it would be over pretty quickly. But it's not. There's a catch: if two Vampires strangle or bite each other, they cancel each other out, and so become mortal again. With the Victim supply kept fresh in this manner, the game can go on for a very long time . . .

MURDER ON ALL FOURS

Props: A pack of playing cards

Preparation: Practise crawling with your eyes shut

A whimsical version of *Murder in the Dark*, *Murder On All Fours* is a game that will leave you in giggling heaps on the floor, and is all the more fun if you are feeling a little tiddly and over-excited. Once again, the Murderer is the person who draws the Ace of Spades. The Detective is whoever draws the Jack of Hearts.

The Detective declares himself and disappears into the bathroom turning off all the lights in the room as he goes. The remaining players, including the Murderer, drop down on all fours, and crawl around the floor, blindly bumping into one another as they go.

The Murderer kills his victim by strangulation. The victim then silently collapses flat on his tummy. The first player to crawl into the victim's prostrate form orders everybody else to freeze, and then crawls off to alert the Detective.

The Detective prods the corpse and interrogates the living (see *Murder in the Dark*) — still frozen on all fours — until he is satisfied that he has identified the criminal. A wrong accusation leads to a forfeit.

ALIBI

Props: A pack of playing cards

Preparation: Read lots of Shakespeare and Agatha Christie, and get into lateral thinking.

Of all the murder games this is the hardest. It requires a mental agility that many party-goers sadly lack, or lose within the course of an evening.

The Murderer and the Detective are selected in the usual way — the Murderer is the player who draws the Ace of Spades, while the Detective is whoever draws the Jack of Hearts.

The Murderer keeps his identity secret, but the Detective steps forward and announces that he has just discovered the body of The Reverend Plunkett-Greene (or whoever) in the library (or wherever) and that The Reverend was murdered at around 11pm (or whenever).

The rest of you — including the Murderer — are suspects, and you must all submit to the Detective's questioning. You can tell whatever tale you like *unless you are the villain.* The Murderer must somehow include in his story two disguised facts: a) that he committed the murder, and b) what he committed it with. This is no mean task.

In answer to the question, 'Where were you at the time of the murder?', suspects might reply as follows:

Great Aunt Beatrix: 'I was nowhere near the library. I was knitting in the parlour. But I did see Cousin Fred sidling along the edge of the house at about 11 pm.'

Cousin Fred now explains: 'I was out badger-spotting. But come to think of it, didn't I see Olive Pilkington turning out the library lights sometime late in the evening?'

Olive Pilkington: 'Oh, well, that's easily explained. I'd gone to look up a quotation from Hamlet. However, just as I turned the lights out, I espied Colonel Mustard looking in through the French windows. He was brandishing a cricket bat of all things.'

Colonel Mustard explains that he was merely practising his swipes. And so on.

The Detective must now consider the evidence and decide who is the culprit. He has to bear in mind that everybody — including the Murderer — is reacting to the accusation of a previous suspect, but that the Murderer is also hinting at his guilt. Just as criminals always return to the scene of their crime, so they also always brag.

In this case, the villain is Olive Pilkington, an unlikely Murderer in her tweed skirt and brogues.

A well-read Detective will pick up on her reference to Hamlet, and will ask: 'What, Olive Pilkington, was the quotation you were looking for?'

To which the erudite but ensnared Miss P replies:

> 'It hath the primal eldest curse upon't,
> A brother's murder!'

And the murder weapon? The cricket bat of course.

This game can shoot off along some interesting tangents, principally because nobody has a clue what's going on. Even the Murderer has to tailor his story to those of the other suspects. It's important, therefore, to give all the suspects a few minutes before the game begins to work out their alibis — the more extravagant the better.

If the Detective accuses the right suspect, he wins a prize. If the Murderer gets away with his crime (and can prove his hints were adequate), he becomes the next Detective.

WHODUNNIT?

Props: None

Preparation: Time for some more lateral thinking

Another murder game for those who have agile criminal minds, and for anyone who's good at lateral thinking.

One of you describes the scene of a crime. Your description includes clues as to what has happened, and plenty of red herrings to confuse the rest of the players.

Here are some examples:

1. Charlotte lies dead in the bath. The radio is on, a tap is running and a bottle of shampoo dribbles onto the floor.

2. A man with a hairy chest lies dead beside a river. A length of rope lies ten yards away from him. The man has a knife in his hand.

The rest of you ask questions until you work out how the person died. (The title *Whodunnit?* is therefore both daft and redundant — but it wasn't my idea.)

In the above cases, the answers are:
1. Charlotte is a spider.
2. The man is Tarzan — his rope snapped.

THE HANGMAN

Props: A piece of string, looped in a noose at one end

Preparation: None

One of you is chosen to be Hangman. The rest of you sit on the floor in a circle, with outstretched forefingers (one per player) meeting in the middle.

The Hangman drops the noose over the raised forefingers and at the cry of 'Death!', or something else equally macabre, he tugs swiftly at the string. Players with quick reactions pull their fingers out of the noose before it tightens; those who are too slow must accept death gracefully and fall back on the floor.

Before too long, the carpet will be strewn with corpses, and only one raised forefinger will remain. Whoever it belongs to deserves a prize and should be awarded one accordingly.

IDENTIFYING THE CORPSE

Props: A blindfold and a selection of disgusting objects (e.g. cold cooked spaghetti, a peeled grape, raw chickens' livers, a string of raw sausages)

Preparation: Nothing can prepare you for this . . .

Not strictly speaking a murder game, but ghoulish enough to be included in this chapter.

A poor unsuspecting individual is singled-out and blind-folded. Various objects are then placed in his hand, which he must identify as parts of the body. A peeled grape, for instance, poses as an excellent eyeball, while a string of sausages can pass for intestines. A plate of cold cooked (oiled) spaghetti is the brain, and chicken livers can be prac-tically any other part of the innards.

If you wish to be truly sadistic, you can force your victim to eat whatever he fails to identify correctly. But remember, the human mind is a fragile thing. You want people to *remember* your party, not to spend the rest of their lives at the shrink's trying to *forget* it.

4

GAMES
for the clever
and the cultured

It may come as a surprise to many that charging about in the dark in a frenzied mixture of excitement and terror is not everybody's idea of fun. For some (especially the elderly and the wise), a more sophisticated form of entertainment is preferable.

For these people, a civilised round of *The Proverb Game* is infinitely more pleasurable than either *Murder in the Dark* or *Murder on all Fours*. Whatever you do, don't try to convince them otherwise — they may, after all , be afraid of the dark.

The games described in the next few pages require wits, so if your guests are alcoholically impaired, or if they are naturally lacking in this department, you may want to try one of the other chapters.

BOTTICELLI

Props: None

Preparation: None

'Who's he?'

It's conceivable that some of your more pickled/ignorant guests may ask this question. Take it as a warning, and banish them to another room for something a little less mentally taxing – *Musical Cushions* is probably about their level.

One of you thinks of a famous person – dead, alive, fictional or non-fictional – and announces the initial letter of his or her name. The task of the remaining players is to guess the full name. If Great Aunt Beatrix is selecting the name, she could easily plump for some obscure missionary from Outer Mongolia, or one of the Lesser Saints, or a character from her favourite soap. Make sure she understands that the person should be known to you all.

You start out with some basic questions:

'Are you alive?'
'Are you fictional?'
'Are you Prussian?'
'Does your name begin with 'C'?'

To which Great Aunt Beatrix, or whoever, must reply with a simple 'Yes' or 'No'. This could be hard for one accustomed to expressing herself in longer sentences.

Knowing your first letter is, say, 'T', and having established the sort of person G.A.B. is thinking of, your cross-examination becomes more probing and precise:

'Are you a Bishop sometimes worn by ballerinas?'
'No.' (She is not Desmond Tutu.)
'Are you the husband of the British Prime Minsiter?'
'No.' (Nor, then, is she Denis Thatcher.)
'Would you like to be?' (What sort of question is that?)
'No.'

By process of elimination, you will eventually discover that
G.A.B. is Tutankhamun, or some other stuffed shirt. Whoever makes the correct guess thinks up the next name.

THE SECRET WORD GAME

Props: None

Preparation: Think up a few suitable words before the party begins

One of you leaves the room while the rest of you think up a word. Any word will do, so long as it's the sort that can be slipped into a conversation easily and unobtrusively.

When the first player is called back in, he must discover the word by asking the rest of you questions, and finding the word in each one of your answers.

If your word were, for example, 'great', the game might go like this:

'How many children have you got?'
'Oh a great many — I've lost count, my dear. One in every port and all that...'
'What do you think of stupid games like this?'
'Well, to be honest I don't indulge myself too often — although there is a great deal to be said for this sort of thing.'

And so on. The longer the answer, the more difficult it will be for the questioner to identify the word. If, however, you choose something obvious like 'elephant' or 'pantheistic', the game is likely to be over rather quickly.

THE DICTIONARY GAME

Props: A dictionary, paper and pencils

Preparation: Take a dictionary to bed with you the night before

If you have ever nurtured an ambition to host one of those TV quiz shows, this one's for you.

Hunt through the dictionary and find the most obscure word. Read it and then spell it out to the other players. If anyone admits to knowing the word (which they will do in nice circles), you will have to look up an alternative.

Having chosen your word — let's say it's 'phalarope' — you now write down the dictionary definition: 'Kind of small wading and swimming bird allied to snipe'. The other players also write down definitions of their own: 'Yellow-fringed girdle worn by belly dancers in North Africa'; 'Toad-eating reptile whose natural habitat is the Upper Amazon'; 'Guinea pig stew, delicacy among indigenous people of Peru'.

These are then handed over to you, the quiz master. Having shuffled all the answers, you read them out in a random order and ask the other players to guess at the correct definition. They get a point for a correct guess, and a further point every time another player chooses their definition. Whoever scores the highest number of points chooses the next word.

NAMES OF

Props: Nimble wits

Preparation: Mental gymnastics

One of those hand-clapping and table-thumping games, where a natural rhythmic ability can be a considerable advantage, and where you'll wish you weren't feeling quite so addled.

A rhythm is set up among all the players — clap clap bang bang is usual — and when everyone has got the hang of it the game begins. Illustration is the only way to explain it:

Clap clap bang bang
Leader: Names of . . .
Clap clap
Leader: Fat men
Clap clap
Leader: Big Daddy.
Clap clap
Player Two: Henry VIII.
Clap clap
Player Three: Demis Roussos.
Clap clap
Player Four: Orson Welles.
Clap clap
Player Five: Ummmmm . . .
Others: OUT!!!

So the game continues, with players dropping out whenever they draw a blank. The place of Leader rotates clockwise, with a new category selected each time.

Some easy categories include: Famous Lovers, Dog Breeds and Film Stars. Really rotten ones are: Chilean Poets, Chinese Towns and Austrian Astronauts.

CAN I COME WITH YOU?

Props: None

Preparation: None

One player states a holiday destination and the luggage he is going to take with him. The rest of the players have to guess by what criterion he is choosing the luggage. It's another of those games which is best explained through illustration:

Player One:'I am going to Blackpool, and I'll take a bucket but not a spade.'
Player Two:(thinks) 'Well, you could have chosen somewhere better . . . if I take a suitcase, but not a trunk, can I come with you?'
Player One: (smug): 'Not this time.'
Player Three:'If I take a camera, but not a film, can I come with you?'
Player One:'Nope.'
Player Four:'If I take a sandwich, but not a cake, can I come with you?'
Player One: 'But of course.'

Player Four, one of those irritating know-alls who you wouldn't want on holiday, even in Blackpool, has caught on. The first player's criterion for picking his luggage is that the items must end with a consonant.

That one's quite easy, but how about these more fiendish categories? Try words of Latin origin, or words of three syllables when translated into French. Those should keep them guessing.

GOING BLANK

Props: None

Preparation: None

A game which takes the form of speedy cross-examination, and which will leave most players jittery and feeling profoundly stupid. Stop here if you feel that way already.

One of you is nominated Inquisitor. Your first job is to think of three categories - Singers, Cats and Kings would do. Next, you gather the rest of the company around you, and jabbing your finger at random individuals you call out your categories. Whoever you are pointing at, must supply the name of a Singer, Cat, King or whatever. Here's how it might go:

Inquisitor: 'Singers!'
Player One: 'Placido Domingo.'
Inquisitor: 'Kings!'
Player Two: 'Louis XIV'
Inquisitor: 'Kings!'
Player Two: 'Juan Carlos.'
Inquisitor: 'Cats!'
Player Three:'Siamese.'
Inquisitor: 'Kings!'
Player Two: 'Me again? Oh blast.'
Inquisitor: 'Never heard of him. You're out.'

Exit Player Two, mumbling that he has been victimised, which is, of course, true.

Speed is of the essence here. Whoever sticks it out to the bitter end becomes the next Inquisitor.

IN COMMON

Props: None

Preparation: Be sure that you (the Inquisitor) have plenty of suitable 'in commons' up your sleeve, otherwise this game will be over very quickly

A variation of *Going Blank*, in which speed is also of the essence. Once again you must appoint an Inquisitor. The game proceeds like this:

Inquisitor: 'What have Fergie and Sarah Brightman in common?'
Player One: 'Husbands called Andrew.'
Inquisitor: 'Correct. What have Mick Jagger and Walt Disney in common?'
Player Two: 'Jerries.'
Inquisitor: 'What have the Beatles and the Bible in common?'
Player Three:'Not much, I should say.'
Inquisitor: 'Wrong! They both have Pauls.'

An alternative way of playing is to rotate the role of Inquisitor, so that when a player gives an answer, it becomes his turn to ask the next question.

THE PROVERB GAME

Props: A Dictionary of Proverbs

Preparation: A doctorate in English

A player is sent out of the room while the others choose a proverb. When the first player is called back, he must try and discover the proverb by asking each of the other players a question in turn. The first answer must include the first word of the proverb, the second must include the second and so on.

Say you choose 'Cold hands, warm heart.' You call the first player back in, and tell him your proverb has four words. The game could then continue like this:

Player One: 'What do you think of the wine you're drinking?'
Player Two: 'Well..it should be more **chambré**. A little cold for my liking. But it's making me merry enough.' (Nice one. The guesser may be fooled into thinking your proverb is 'Merry meet, merry part'.)
Player One: 'Do you like it?' (Using the same question is a good ploy.)
Player Three: 'Oh, I think it's excellent. It wins hands down with me.'
Player One: (baffled) 'What's the weather been like in your part of the world?'
Player Four: 'Umm...well, warm actually.' (A giveaway.)

If Player One has an ounce of intelligence he should be able to figure out the proverb by now. And when he does, somebody else takes his place.

Useful proverbs include:

- ★ East, west, home's best
- ★ The proof of the pudding is in the eating
- ★ Barking dogs seldom bite
- ★ Cold hands, warm heart
- ★ Look before you leap
- ★ Let sleeping dogs lie
- ★ Man cannot live by bread alone
- ★ First come, first served
- ★ Beauty's in the eye of the beholder
- ★ A bird in hand is worth two in a bush
- ★ A rolling stone gathers no moss
- ★ Absence makes the heart grow fonder
- ★ Marry in haste and repent at leisure

FIZZ BUZZ

Props: None

Preparation: A doctorate in Maths

How I hate this game. It tests your mathematical powers (or lack of) and gives you real brain strain. I can't see why it's so popular. But it is.

Players sit in a circle and call out numbers in turn — the first player calls out 'One', the second 'Two' and so on until you get to the seventh player. He must substitute the word 'Fizz' for seven. Thereafter, every number which contains a seven (like 17 or 27), or which is a multiple of seven (14, 21, 28), is also taboo and must be replaced with 'Fizz'. Players who pause or stumble are eliminated.

That's the easy version.

You can make matters harder by introducing a new element — the word 'Buzz', which replaces five and multiples of five. This also means that any number that contains or is a multiple of both five and seven is substituted with 'Fizz-Buzz!'

It doesn't take long before one sharp-minded individual is left in the game. He should be given a prize (or a forfeit, if you think that's what he deserves.)

TABOO

Props: None

Preparation: None

One of you is selected to think of a much-used word, and to declare that word taboo. This player now asks each of the other players a question. They must reply sensibly, without hesitating and without using the taboo word.

Anybody who errs is eliminated from the game, and the questions continue until only one player — the winner — remains. He chooses the next taboo word. Suitable words include: is, you, the, a, but, and, I.

A more arduous version of the game bans the use of a chosen letter. Personally, I think this is too much like hard work to be any fun. But you can agree to differ.

CHICKEN EGG BACON

Props: None

Preparation: None

An intellectually invigorating game which anyone can play.

One of you thinks of a word and calls it out. The next player follows with another word, connected in some way with the first. The third player responds to the second player's word in the same manner and so the game continues until some poor idiot falters or seizes up completely.

The connections might go something like this:

Player One: 'Salt!'
Player Two: 'Pepper!'
Player Three: 'Corn!'
Player Four: 'Foot!'
Player One: 'Leg!'
Player Two: 'Arm!'
Player Three: 'Elbow!'
Player Four: 'Tennis!'

The trick is to play very fast and to be ruthless with anyone who breaks the chain. Give them three lives and then make them pay a forfeit.

LAST AND FIRST

Props: None

Preparation: Think up a few suitable categories before the game begins

Another game which should be played at high speed if it's to be any fun.

You start off by thinking up a category — Towns, Writers, Animals, Root Vegetables, for example. This done, the first player calls out a word belonging to the category. Player number two must swiftly follow on with another word from the same category, which begins with the last letter of the previous word. The next player then calls out a word beginning with the last letter of the second word.

If the category were cars, the chain of words might be: 'Jaguar', 'Rover', 'Renault', 'Talbot', 'Toyota', 'Alfa Romeo' and so on.

The game continues until someone repeats a word, stumbles, pauses or makes a word up. He is eliminated, another category is chosen and the remaining players play on until only one remains — the winner.

THE PRINCE OF WALES HAS LOST HIS HAT

Props: Table, chair per player

Preparation: This is a complicated game so make sure you know the rules before trying to explain it to your guests; practise with the family first — you need two or three people who understand it

So you thought explaining cricket to a Frenchman was difficult. Try explaining this game to a group of inebriated friends...

   Players sit round a table and count off clockwise from one until everybody has a number, the game then proceeds like this:

One: 'The Prince of Wales has lost his hat, and number four has found it.'
Four: 'No sir, Not I, sir!'
One: 'Then who, sir?'
Four: 'Eight, sir.'
Eight: 'No sir. Not I, sir!'
Four: 'Then who, sir?'
Eight: 'Three, sir.'
Three: 'No sir. Not I, sir!'
Eight: 'Then who, sir?'

   All of this happens at high speed. Anyone who stumbles or changes the formula in any way has to move down to the last chair round the table. In a game of eight players, this would mean that if, for instance, Number Five bungled he would move to Number Eight's chair. The original Number Eight would then move into seven's chair, seven would become six, and six would move into the chair vacated by five (in this instance, four, three, two and one stay put). With players changing seats and numbers in this way, it's only too easy to get in a muddle.

If, however, your friends are teetotallers, or simply on the ball, you could play the advanced version of the game. Here, the first four players are named Matthew, Mark, Luke and John, while remaining players are numbered. The game would then go something like this:

Matthew: *'The Prince of Wales has lost his hat, and number Six has found it.'*
Six: 'No Matthew. Not I, Matthew!'
Matthew: 'Then who, sir?'
Six: 'Luke, Matthew.'
Luke: 'No sir, Not I, sir.'
Six: 'Then who, Luke?'
Luke: 'John, sir.'
John: 'No Luke. Not I, Luke!'
Luke:'Then who, John?'
John:'Seven, Luke.'
Seven: 'No John. Not, I John.'

And so on, until you are all exhausted, or until a pre-arranged time limit is up. As you can see, Matthew and co have to be addressed by their names, whereas numbers are addressed as 'Sir' (irrespective of sex, I fear.) Any slip, and the duffer moves to the last chair, the occupant of the last chair moves up a place, etcetera.

Terrific fun, if you can only explain it . . .

5
GAMES
for exhibitionists

Everyone loves to show off. And don't be fooled into thinking it's just the amateur actors and extroverts who get a buzz out of making a spectacle of themselves. More often than not it's the quiet ones who throw themselves most vigorously into the games in this chapter — especially after a drink or three.

Included here are the best of the acting games, for which everyone will doubtless have their own set of rules. This can lead to general confusion, and if you want to avoid tears, tantrums and Nasty Scenes In The Kitchen, you should lay down the law firmly at the very outset; they're in *your* house, so they must play *your* way.

If they don't, it could be time for a round of *The Wind and the Leaves*, which you'll find on page 120

THE GAME

Props: A pencil and paper (for one player) and three rooms

Preparation: Give the player who is writing the list plenty of time for inspiration

Some people mistakenly refer to this game as *Charades*. It is not. *The Game* is the Prince of Parlour Games, and acquired its name because back in Victorian times it was *the* game to play. Everyone knew and loved it.

The principle is simple. There are two teams and a list of titles. Players take it in turns to mime a title which their team members have to guess. Whoever guesses correctly mimes the next title, and so on until one of the teams has mimed its way through the entire list ahead of the other team.

To begin, one of the players is sent to a quiet corner — the kitchen, the lavatory or wherever — where he or she compiles a list of titles of books, plays, films, songs and so on. (This is an excellent job for an emotional cripple like your pathologically shy third cousin, or an elderly guest like your great grandmother.)

The list might include:

War and Peace
Roget's *Thesaurus.*
Armageddon
Amadeus
Kramer versus Kramer
Dr Zhivago
Pride and Prejudice
Cagney and Lacey
Tosca

You get the idea.
The rest of the party splits into two teams, each of which

gathers in a separate room. At the word 'Go!' one member of each team is dispatched to the kitchen/loo to discover the first title on the list. This person must then race back to his or her team, and *mime* the title. Certain visual aids are allowed at this juncture:

A book: You hold your hands out, palms uppermost, little fingers touching.
A song: Press one hand to your heart, thrust the other hand heavenwards, and affect a soupy smile.
An opera: An exaggerated version of the same.
A film: Crank an imaginary movie camera.
A TV programme: Draw a rectangle in the air.
A play: Draw the outline of stage curtains in the air.

Other visual aids include:

★ Holding up fingers to indicate the number of words in the title, and also to indicate which of those words is being acted out.
★ Slapping your forearm with an appropriate number of fingers to indicate syllables.
★ Cupping your ear with your hand to indicate that the correct word *sounds like* another word you are about to act.
★ Holding up your thumb and forefinger, to indicate a short word (it, the, a, but, and . . .)
★ Tapping your nose to indicate your team has got the word.

As soon as the team guesses the full title, another member (usually whoever came up with the correct answer), races to the kitchen where he or she is given the next title on the list. The game continues in this manner until one of the teams completes the list and wins.

Another way of playing *The Game* is to dispense with the teams and simply have individuals taking it in turns to act out titles and so on for the rest of the party to guess. This lacks the element of competition, so is generally not as exciting.

CHARADES 1

Props: None

Preparation: Prepare yourself for a barrage of 'That's not the way we play Charades . . .'

Charades can be a contentious subject at parties, as most people will have their own idea about how it should be played. This version is the TRUE version, and let nobody try to persuade you otherwise. I gather it's the one *they* play at Balmoral, so it must be all right.

Draw up two teams. Each side now thinks up a word of two to four syllables, with each syllable making a word (approximately) of its own. You might, for example, choose 'bombastic' which could be broken down into 'bomb', 'ass' and 'tick', or 'truculant' which makes 'truck', 'yule' and 'ant'.

Team 'A' then mimes its chosen word syllable by syllable, and finally in full, to Team 'B'. The way I have always played it is with the whole team acting en masse, but you may prefer to have individual players act out each of the syllables and then have whole team act out the word. Ham actors will have a ball, and this is how they might deal with 'bombastic'.

1. Bomb The actors are going about their daily business when suddenly they leap in the air and fall dead on the ground. Scope for writhing, gasping and dramatic last rites.

2. Ass The actors crawl about on all-fours, hands flapping at the sides of their heads to indicate that they have large ears. Alternatively, they could walk in, drop their trousers or lift their skirts and moon at their opponents, although this might be deemed a trifle puerile in some circles.

3. Tick The actors either look at their watches or twitch.

4.Bombastic They strut around pretending to be Colonel Gadaffi.

When Team B has guessed the word, it becomes their turn to leave the room, choose a word and then act it out in the same way.

Most people will enjoy this version of *Charades* more than any other, principally because it's more fun and less embarrassing to act in teams than alone. Any objections will come from the prima donnas who prefer to strut the stage solo.

CHARADES 2

Props: A pencil and paper per team

Preparation: Teams will need ten minutes or so to think up their lists

This is a combination of *The Game* and *Charades 1*.

Two teams are formed and gather in separate rooms. Each compiles a list of books, plays, songs, operas, films and so on. You should think up one title for each member of the opposing team. Suitable examples are given in *The Game* (page 58).

With their lists completed, the two teams reassemble in the drawing room and take it in turn to call over a member of the opposing team and give him one of the titles from their list. He then mimes the title before the assembled company, while his team tries to guess what it is. As with *The Game*, certain visual aids are allowed, and these are as described on page 58.

The great thing about *Charades 2* is that you can tailor your titles to the members of the rival team. Nasty ones – *Jude the Obscure* and *Mrs Beeton's Cookery and Household Management*, for instance – can be given to poseurs and people you don't like; while the easy ones – *Jaws 4* and *The Magic Flute* – are kept for the timid, the lonely, the lame or anyone else for whom you feel a measure of compassion.

There are no winners or losers in this game, although you can, if you wish to spice things up, award points and prizes for the best performances.

SOLO CHARADES

Props: A pencil and paper per player and a hat

Preparation: None

This is a variation on the above and is generally less satisfactory because there is a chance that titles will be duplicated.

Everybody writes the name of a book/play/film/song or whatever on a scrap of paper, folds it up and places it in a hat or some other receptacle. Players then take it in turns to dip a hand into the hat and pluck out one of the titles, which they must then mime to the rest of the company.

Not as fun as the team-acting games, although actors and show-offs would have you think otherwise.

NEBUCHADNEZZAR

Props: None

Preparation: None

A learned version of *Charades 1*, this is played by the intelligentsia in north Oxford drawing rooms.

Again, you split into two teams, each of which thinks of a famous person. The first team then acts out its chosen name, letter by letter, using the initial letter of another famous name in each case. You can either choose to act singly or as a team, depending upon your acting skills (or lack of) and courage.

For Bach you might mime Bardot (lots of pouting and posing), Abraham (praying and conversing with the heavens), Columbus (looking through telescopes and planting flag poles) and Helen of Troy (more pouting and posing).

As with *Charades 1*, the team then closes its pantomime with the whole word. In this case the actor or actors might pretend to be playing the organ. If and when the other team has guessed the name, it becomes their turn to act while the first team guesses.

THE MANNER OF THE WORD

Props: None

Preparation: None

Yet another *Charades* variant. One player is banished from the room. The rest of you put your heads together and agree on an adjective — lasciviously, sleepily, angrily, meticulously, for example.

The exiled player returns to the room and tries to discover the adjective by firing questions at everybody. They must reply *in the manner of the word*, i.e. lasciviously, sleepily, angrily, meticulously or whatever. if the adjective were 'angrily', the game might go something like this:

Tom: 'What did you have for dinner this evening?'
Dick: 'How dare you ask me such an impertinent question!'
Tom: 'Where are you going on holiday this year?'
Harry: 'Holiday? Hah — fat chance of getting a holiday this year.'

If you are all drunk it may well prove difficult for the first player to work out what the adjective is, but that adds to the challenge of the game. When the adjective has been dis-covered, another player is sent out, and the game goes on until everyone tires of it.

MÉTIERS

Props: Optional

Preparation: Practise in front of the mirror before everyone arrives

Métiers — named after the French for job or occupation — is a game which will thrill the fantasists among you. It's also extremely funny.

The idea is simple. Each player dreams up a *métier* and takes it in turn to act it out before the others. Some players will really go to town and you'll get some memorable performances — portly gentlemen as air hostesses, elderly matrons as Sumo wrestlers . . .

Some people may not wish to make fools of themselves, but this doesn't matter at all. They'll have enough fun watching the rest of you, and will only be miserable and spoil the fun if forced to perform.

At the end of the show you can call a vote for the wittiest effort, and give the winner a prize.

THE SHERBORNE GAME

Props: None (generally speaking)

Preparation: Nothing can prepare you for this

So called because I played it at school, and haven't discovered an alternative name. This is an acting version of
Chinese Whispers and is one of the best games I know.

Two teams are formed, one of which leaves the room. The
other team (Team A) then decides upon a scene and selects
one of its number to act it out.

Possible scenes include:

★ Buying an underground ticket, travelling down the escal-
 ator, boarding the train, swinging from the handle above
 your head as the train moves along and falling over when
 it stops.
★ Baking bread.
★ Putting on make-up, getting dressed, hailing a taxi and
 going to the disco.
★ Bathing a baby, powdering its bottom, putting on its
 nappy, giving it a bottle and putting it to bed.

The exiled team (Team B) sends a single member back into
the room. He sits, watches a member of Team A mime their
chosen scene and endeavours to remember it. A second
member of Team B is sent in, and the first Team B player acts
his version of the scene to him. The second player then acts it
out for the third member of his team.

The game proceeds until every member of Team B has seen
and repeated the mime, which, by this stage, is likely to bear
little resemblance to the original version. The last Team B
member has the unenviable task of guessing what the mime is
all about. This done, the teams swop places and the game
goes on . . .

DUMB CRAMBO

Props: None

Preparation: None

A game for a fairly small party. The players divide into two teams, and one team (Team A) leaves the room.

Team B chooses a word, calls Team A back into the room and then announces a word which *rhymes* with their chosen word. If, for example, the chosen word were 'bone' they might announce the word 'loan'.

Team A are allowed three guesses in which to discover Team B's word, and they have to present their guesses in mime. If therefore, they decided the word were 'moan', they would all beat their breasts, grimace and so forth. But no sound effects. In this case, they've guessed wrong, and their efforts are greeted with boos and hisses. If they hit on the right word before their three turns are up, Team B applauds them and they win a point.

The teams then swop roles, and at the end of the session, whichever has the most points wins.

DRAMA LESSONS

Props: None

Preparation: Pull faces in the mirror

The ultimate in acting lessons, this game is rather like one of those trendy actors' workshops. It is likely to terrify your more self-conscious guests, and they may well refuse an invitation to your next party. Extroverts and drama students will love it.

One person is designated Director, and the rest of the

guests line up before him. The Director's first job is to lay down the rules of the game. This means he has to decide whether his team of actors (the rest of you) should be allowed to speak, or whether they are to be limited to facial expressions, actions, mime, or whatever.

With the rules established, the Director now orders everyone to act out a variety of feelings and emotions — excitement, panic, love, terror, anguish, boredom. In each case, whoever puts on the most convincing display wins an Oscar. At the end of the game (it can be as long or as short as you like), you add up your Oscars, and whoever has the most is proclaimed the winner.

CONVERSATION

Props: None

Preparation: Practise making small talk

You will all need a good general knowledge to enjoy this game, so stick to *Sardines* and *Musical Cushions* if it's lacking.

Two of you leave the room and decide upon two famous characters — real or fictional, dead or alive — whose identities you then assume. Returning to the room, you launch into the conversation you imagine your two characters would have. The remaining players have to work out who the characters are.

Anyone who thinks they have guessed *both* names joins discretely into the conversation, saying things that are appropriate to the secret identities of the two characters.

The game ends when everyone has correctly guessed the two identities.

By way of a footnote. . . Characters need not know, or have known, each other, but it does help if they have something in common. Oliver Twist might not have a lot to say to Mozart, but Michael Jackson just might. . .

CARRIER BAG

Props: Carrier bags (one per team) and assorted objects.

Preparation: Before everyone arrives, you should fill a number of carrier bags with the assorted objects — five or six for each bag

Players are divided into teams of three or four. Each team is given a bag of objects which it uses to devise a mini drama.
    Here are the sort of things you might put in the bags:

★ An elastic band, a teabag, a book, an American Express card and a lipstick.
★ A bikini, a pencil, a toy car, a piece of string and a plaster.
★ A torch, a flower, a cube of sugar, a pair of sunglasses and a bag of rice.

    The more absurd the combination, the better. It will get people using their imaginations.
    With the contents of the first carrier bag, one of the sketches might go like this:

    A woman walks on stage, sits down at a table and begins to apply her lipstick. She is followed in by a man bearing a cup of tea which he gives her before dropping on to one knee and declaring his passion for her. A second man bursts through the door waving a book in his hand. He races over to the first man and beats him about the head with the book. Digging into her pocket, the woman finds an elastic band. She plucks the teabag out of the cup and catapults it slap into the eye of the assailant. She then pays for her tea (with the American Express card) and leaves the room.

    When all the teams have performed, a vote is taken on the best drama. The winners are given a prize.

THE DRESSING UP GAME

Props: Two outrageous sets of clothes

Preparation: Clear the largest room in the house

This is one of those games which will leave your sides aching from too much laughter. You will have to raid Great Aunt Beatrix's attic if it's to go off with a bang. Ladies' clothes tend to raise more laughs, so you should include in each set a pair of stilettoes (large), a dress (voluminous), a bra (jumbo-size), a hat and a hand bag. Wigs are also a good idea, if you can lay your hands on a couple.

Put the clothes in two piles at the end of a large room and divide your players into two teams, ensuring that the blind, the lame and the halt are fairly distributed.

At the word 'Go!', the first player from each team races down to the other end of the room and puts on one of the sets of clothes. Thus attired, they run (or hobble) back to their teams, clasping wigs, handbags and errant bras, and then return to leave the clothes where they found them.

The game proceeds like a relay race, with each player donning and discarding the clothes in turn. The first team to finish wins.

You do need space to play *The Dressing Up Game* properly, so if the weather's good you might prefer to take it into the garden. Though what the neighbours will think, I don't know . . .

NEWSPAPER FANCY DRESS

Props: A newspaper and a dozen pins per player

Preparation: None

Budding couturiers will excel here.

Give each player a newspaper, some pins and ten minutes in which to fashion a costume. It can be a classic Chanel or something more avant-garde. No artistic constraints are imposed.

When the ten minutes are up, the players saunter down the catwalk à la Marie Helvin in their creations. The best effort wins a prize.

HATS

Props: A newspaper and a dozen pins per player

Preparation: None

A less amusing version of *Newspaper Fancy Dress*, but a useful standby if you have elderly or bashful guests who don't fancy themselves as mannequins.

Once more, you give everybody a newspaper and a dozen pins. Each player makes a hat, and the most stylish effort wins a prize.

TRAIN COMPARTMENT

Props: Two chairs

Preparation: You'll need a few minutes to think up some good phrases

The game calls upon the noble and declining art of conversation. Natural wit and garrulousness is essential for this to be truly amusing, and it won't work if your party is made up of strong silent types.

Send a couple of loquacious extroverts out of the room, and while they are thus exiled the rest of you think of a couple of sentences. 'Have you ever eaten jellied eel?', 'I once had a wart on the end of my nose', 'Do you always smell like that?', 'My mother told me never to talk to strange men/women' and so on.

Once you have come up with a couple of gems, call the two players back in one by one and give them a sentence each, which they must not divulge to the other. They now have to act out a sort of brief encounter in the first class carriage of a train, and *somehow* include their given phrase in the conversation.

At the end of the game you can call a vote to decide who achieved this most skillfully. The winner should be awarded a prize.

6
GAMES
for after
(a large) dinner

OK, so you've worked your way through a magnificent five-course feast, and the last thing you want to do is cavort uproariously around the drawing room. Just heaving yourself up from the table could be a problem, so games seem quite out of the question.

Actually, nothing could be further from the truth. Dining rooms are great places for playing parlour games, and there are a number of after-dinner games, many of which can be played at the table and most of which should not disturb the digestion.

Among these, *Racing Demon* alone should, perhaps, be approached with a little caution. Although it is reputed to be the Queen Mother's *absolute favourite*, it is not a *nice* game. It brings out the worst in the gentlest of people, and has been the cause of many a black eye and broken friendship.

Don't say I didn't warn you!

CONSEQUENCES

Props: A pencil and paper per player

Preparation: None

Consequences is very childish and very amusing. It has to be one of the least sophisticated of parlour games, yet intelligent adults have been known to spend hours sniggering over it.

The idea of the game is to write stories to which each player contributes a sentence, without knowing what the other players have written. The results are almost always absurdly funny.

Each player is given a pencil and paper, and instructed to write down the name of a female. This done, everyone folds their paper to conceal what they have written, and passes it on to the player on their left, who must then provide the name of a male character. The process is repeated, following a set formula, until each paper carries a complete story.

Traditionally the stories go something like this:

A female character (Nancy Reagan)
Met a male character (Fidel Castro)
Where they met (In the lingerie department of Marks & Spencer)
What he did (Danced a reel)
What she did (Stood on her head)
He said ('It's hot in here')
She said ('I must catch the next train')
The consequence was (The Stock Market crash)
What the world said ('Don't drink and drive')

When all the stories have been composed, you take it in turns to read them out. The game is then repeated over and over until it ceases to amuse..

PICTURE CONSEQUENCES

Props: A pencil and paper per player

Preparation: None

This game is even less sophisticated than *Consequences*.

Players are again given a paper and pencil. The object here is to draw characters. Players contribute a part of the drawing, without seeing what the other players have drawn.

Each of you starts out by drawing a head at the top of your piece of paper. You then fold the paper, concealing your masterpiece, and pass it to your neighbour on your left who, in turn, draws a torso. The next player along contributes legs and feet.

When all the pictures are completed, you unfold the paper and giggle at the consequences.

THE POETRY GAME

Props: A pencil and paper per player

Preparation: Read some poems beforehand, so you get a feel for scansion (some people never will)

This can sound high minded. It isn't. *The Poetry Game* is simply the best of the consequences games, and you don't have to be a budding bard to enjoy it.

Everyone sits down with a pencil and paper and writes a line of verse, either their own ('My name is Bertie the Banana') or somebody else's ('Shall I compare thee to a summer's day?'). They then pass their paper (without folding it over) to their neighbour who writes a second line.

The poems develop in this fashion until they reach a set length (eight lines works well). Having written the final lines, the players pass on the papers once more, and each writes a moral for one of the poems.

As a child, my mother was involved in the following verse, which she will recite to this day:

The Dame stood in the kitchen
Wearing her OBE
Concocting horrid dishes
Of frogs and pars-e-lee
When on the table the telephone rang
The Dame she fell with a terrible bang
And spoilt her dainty fricassee
Alack, alack! Ah me, ah me!

MORAL: Wearing your medals won't impress
*   If it ruins your food and makes a mess.*

Unlike *Consequences*, you don't fold the paper. Inspiration flows with greater ease if you can read what has gone before. And don't worry if you know nothing about stanzas, scansion and limping iambics. Doggerel and lame verse are much funnier than polished poetics.

TELEGRAMS

Props: A pencil and paper per player

Preparation: None

There are several ways of playing this game. Here is the correct version.

Pluck a word at random from a book, newspaper or dictionary — for example 'apples'. Everyone then composes a telegram using the letters in the order that they appear in the word.

In this case you might come up with: 'Arriving Paddington. Please leave empty suitcase' or something much better if the muse is on form (mine wasn't). Players all read out their efforts, a vote is taken and the best (i.e. the most ridiculous) telegram wins a prize.

UP JENKINS

Props: A coin

Preparation: Clear the table of breakables

Two teams line up opposite each other on either side of a table. Team A is given a coin, which it passes from hand to hand under the table (Middle-aged men with wandering hands should be slotted in between respectable matrons like the vicar's wife and a grandmother.)

When the captain of Team B cries 'Up Jenkins!', the members of Team A must bring their hands up from under the table, and hold them fists clenched — the coin is in one of the fists.

The captain of Team B then commands 'Down Jenkins!' at which point, the raised hands are slapped palms down on the table. All of Team A should look as guilty as possible so as to bamboozle Team B, whose task it is to identify the hand that hides the coin.

They can do this either by eliminating the hands they *don't* think are hiding the coin, or by swooping straight in for the kill. In both cases, if they are right, they win a point; if they are wrong, Team A wins a point and plays on until Team B guesses correctly. The teams then swop roles, and the game continues until everyone gets bored or thirsty. The points are added up at the end so that one of the teams emerges victorious.

DONKEY

Props: None

Preparation: None

I first played this after a sumptuous dinner; everyone was slumped or wedged in chairs, unable to move. A round of *Donkey* was all we could manage.

The aim is to build words, with each player adding a letter and trying, at the same time, not to be the person who completes the word.

The first player thinks of a letter. The player on his or her left then thinks of a word that begins with that letter, and adds the second letter. The next player must now think of a word that begins with the two given letters, and add the third. Here's an example:

Player One: 'D' (Thinking of 'donkey')
Player Two: 'D-I' (Thinking of 'dictator')
Player Three: 'D-I-Z' (Thinking of 'dizzy')
Player Four: 'D-I-Z-Z' (Also thinking of 'dizzy')
Player Five: 'D-I-Z-Z-oh blast . . . ' (Loses a life)

Player Five loses a life because he was forced to complete a word.

Each player must have a word in mind as he builds on to the letters that have gone before, and may be challenged by another player who suspects foul play. If the challenged player was simply bluffing and cannot declare a word, he loses a life; if he can, his challenger loses a life. Everyone has three lives, and the winner is whoever survives to the end.

BLACK MAGIC

Props: None

Preparation: None

Black Magic requires little or no effort from most of the assembled company, and is therefore another useful game for when you have gorged excessively.

Two players who know the game are chosen. One of them leaves the room; the second player then asks the rest of the party to choose an object in the room, for example the cheese plant in the corner. This done, the first player is called back in and, as if by magic, identifies the chosen object.

Player Two: 'Is it the carriage clock?'
Player One: (dramatic pause . . .)'No'.
Player Two: 'Is it the Picasso?'
Player One: 'No.'
Player Two: 'Is it Cousin Fred's shoe?'
Player Two: 'No'
Player Two: 'Is it the cheese plant?'
Player One: (with a flourish) 'Yes!'

Gasps of astonishment from those who have never played before. *How could Player One know?* The answer is simple. The object referred to by Player Two immediately before the cheese plant was Cousin Fred's shoe — which is black. Therein lies Player One's clue, and hence the name *Black Magic*.

Clever, heh?

THE CLAIRVOYANT

Props: None

Preparation: Two minutes in which two of you agree on your secret code . . .

Another game in which two of you play on everybody else's alcohol-induced incredulity.

Having agreed on your 'secret code', one of the two (the Clairvoyant) leaves the room, closing the door firmly behind him. The second player (the Clairvoyant's Assistant) now gathers everyone else together, and asks each person to place one of their own personal belongings on the table — a brooch, a tie, a watch, for example.

This done, the Assistant calls to the Clairvoyant through the closed door: 'Clairvoyant, tell us the articles placed on this table by each of the present company. . . What, for instance, is our kind host's article?'

To which the clever Clairvoyant correctly replies: 'A watch, I believe.' (General amazement all round.)

'Next, tell me what Great Aunt Beatrix placed on the table.'

'A necklace.'

Right again. The game continues in this fashion, with the duped players more impressed each time. Eventually some bright spark will pick up on the secret code which is, of course, that the first letter of the first word of the question, is also the initial letter of the article.

HONEST INJUN

Props: Playing cards and money or match sticks for placing your bets

Preparation: None

A bastardized version of poker, requiring no skill whatsoever.

A pack of cards is shuffled, and one card passed face down to each player. The dealer calls 'Injuns!', and each player picks up his card, licks its back and sticks it to his forehead — all this without looking at it.

The players now begin to bet on whether their card is higher or lower than the other cards displayed. A little informed guessing can pay off here; by the law of averages, if most of the other cards are low, yours could well be high. And vice versa.

You can bet with money, matches or whatever takes your fancy. And if you want to improve your chances of winning (i.e. you want to cheat), sit opposite someone with glasses — you'll see your own card reflected in the lenses.

SCISSORS

Props: A pair of scissors

Preparation: Be sure that two or three people know the trick of the game

A wonderfully restful game which requires that everybody is seated in a comfortable chair — not around a table.

A pair of scissors are passed round the circle. As you hand them to your neighbour, you must state whether you are passing on the scissors 'crossed' or 'uncrossed'. Those who aren't in the know, will assume you are referring to the blades — whether they are open or closed. You aren't. You are referring to your ankles or legs.

There is much amusement to be had from this game if you know what's going on, not least of all when another player thinks he has twigged, passes you the open scissors with a triumphant 'Crossed!' and looks positively apoplectic when you reply with a smug 'NO!'.

It can take some people hours (literally) to catch on to the fact that it is legs that are being crossed and uncrossed, not the scissors, and you may need to resort to some pretty exaggerated flinging of one leg over the other, lest the game should drag on late into the night.

I LOVE MY LOVE

Props: None

Preparation: None

Players take it in turn to complete the sentence 'I love my love because he/she is...' with adjectives beginning with successive letters in the alphabet. The game is rather weedy if you stick to the conventionally sugary adjectives – 'amiable', 'beautiful', 'courteous', 'dashing' – and you'll have much more fun with 'argumentative', 'bossy', 'churlish', 'demonic' and so on.

Players who cannot think of an adjective beginning with the next letter of the alphabet drop out. The next player starts again with A, and the game goes on until a single player survives.

Matters can be complicated by forbidding repetition. In other words, once you go back to the beginning of the alphabet you cannot use 'argumentative', 'bossy', etc. again. You must come up with new alternatives – 'ancient', 'bald' or whatever.

An even more sophisticated version requires players to think of three or more adjectives at a time, to complete a longer sentence. An example here would be, 'I love my love because he is vexing, vigorous and vegetarian.'

Players who are eliminated in the early rounds may be made to pay forfeits.

CHINESE WHISPERS

Props: At least one ear per player

Preparation: Practise whispering sweet nothings to your beloved

Deaf people like your grandfather may need to be told — very kindly — that this game is not for them. They invariably whisper exceedingly loudly, thus spoiling the game for the other players.

Chinese Whispers is best played round a table with at least six players — the more the merrier. One player thinks up a line. Any line will do. It can be lifted from Oscar Wilde or Barbara Cartland, or it can be wholly original. In nasty circles it is generally a bitchy remark about one of the other players, so I'm told.

The line is whispered from player to player, and then announced by the last player in the form that it reaches him. The first player then announces his original line, and you all fall about laughing.

Skilful and practised players will start the game with long sentences, jam-packed with sub-clauses, and whispered to their neighbours at high speed.

TOWN AND COUNTRY

Props: A pencil and paper per player

Preparation: None

First you must decide on a list of categories — about six or eight will do. Suggested ideas are Towns, Countries, Animals, Novelists, Items of Clothing, Colours.

Each player writes the list of categories across the top of his sheet of paper. A letter is then chosen at random, and the players race to find a word for each category beginning with that letter. The first to do so shouts 'Stop!' at which point all scribbling must cease.

Everyone then goes through their answers, scoring two points for any word that nobody else has thought of, and one point for any other. The player who finished first also gets a bonus of three points.

A new letter is then chosen, and the game continues. The winner is whoever amasses the highest score.

You can adapt this game to suit your group of players — categories such as Lithuanian Street Names, Names of Flowers (in Latin), Revolutionary Leaders and Saints are quite legitimate, if a little obscure. *À chacun son goût.*

PINOCHLE

Props: A pack of card per six players

Preparation: The less preparation the better — if you try to explain this to people you'll all get in a terrible muddle. The best way to go about the game is ensure you have at least one other player who knows the rules. Let the rest of them learn by trial and error — it won't take long!

Pronounced *Peaknuckle*, this is a game requiring wits, competitiveness and a little malice. The aim is to get rid of your hand first — and to stop other players from doing likewise. Not nearly as hard as it sounds, and beginners should only take 10—15 minutes to pick it up.

You need at least three players and a pack of cards — two packs, if you have more than six players; three if you have more than twelve, and so on.

Everyone is dealt seven cards. The remaining cards are placed face down in a pile in the middle of the table. The dealer then takes the top card and lies it face up next to the pile.

If this card were, for the sake of argument, the four of hearts, Player One — usually to the dealer's left — would now have to place either another heart or another four from his hand on top of it. If he cannot, he takes a card from the pile, so increasing both his hand and his chances of losing. However, if he's lucky and he has a four of spades, say, he jubilantly slams it on to the table. Player Two, in this case, would now need to find either another spade, or another four. Again, failure to do so leads to the penalty of taking a card from the middle.

There are a number of cards which bedevil this seemingly simple game. If you use these cards, the next player may come to grief and you can then trounce him.

★ *Ace:* This changes the direction of play, from clockwise to anticlockwise, or vice versa.

★ *Two:* A tricky one. If, for instance, Player One plays a two, then Player Two must do likewise (he does not have the usual option of playing a card from the same suit). If he *cannot* play a two, his penalty is to pick up two cards from the pile in the middle. If, however, he can play a two, then Player Three must do likewise. Failure to do so means that *this* player's penalty is to take four cards from the middle. If, however, Player Three can also provide a two, then Player Four must try to do so as well. By this time, the penalty for failure is six cards from the middle. The jinx is broken when a player cannot play a two, and is obliged to take the cards from the middle.

★ *Eight:* This means the next player is passed over.

★ *Jack:* Can be played in lieu of any card and at any time except after a two.

★ *Queen:* If you play a Queen, you can also play any other cards of the same suit in the same go.

If you make a false move, or respond too slowly to any of these cards, your opponents will shout 'Penalty card!' and lumber you with a card from the middle.

They will also be anxious to catch you out if you're close to winning, and have only one card left. If anyone spots you in this happy position, they will also cry 'Penalty card!' and you'll then be up to two cards again. You can preempt this by shouting 'Pinochle' when you get to the last-card stage. Remember, however, that the other players will then gang up and do their level best to stop you. Best policy is to play sneakily, concealing the number of cards in your palm. And to resist that smirk which informs the enemy that you are about to win.

Points are added up at the end of the game. Count five for any of the special cards, one for any of the others left in your hand. Several rounds of *Pinochle* will give an overall winner — the person with the fewest points.

RACING DEMON

Props: A pack of (old and unloved) cards per player

Preparation: Clear the table, sharpen up your wits and make sure everyone understands the house rules

Racing Demon is no fun unless you have at least six players, although you can play with as few as three. Each player must have a pack of cards — don't use your best one, as they're liable to get mangled during the course of this game, which is invariably accompanied by wild lunging, tearing at the cards and screams of 'Mine!' Another word of warning — *Racing Demon* is a vicious game, and, like *Croquet*, it can end in tears. Don't blame me.

Each player deals himself 13 cards — his *demon* — and places these face up in a pile in front of him. A further four cards are then laid face up in a row next to the *demon*. The player keeps the remaining cards in his hand. His aim is to get rid of his demon before anybody else gets rid of theirs, and to pick up as many points as he can on the way.

This is achieved by:

★ Building single-suit sets (Ace up to King) in the centre of the table.

★ Building on the four upturned cards in descending order and alternate colours.

At the word 'Go!' players quickly examine their four upturned cards. If there is an ace, it is pushed into the middle of the table where it will be built upon. Its place is filled by the top card in the demon.

Players then work their way through the cards in their hand, repeatedly turning them up in threes so that they see only every third card, and scanning the middle of the table to see if there is a place for it there, or on the row of four cards. Cards from the rows can also be pushed in the middle, and replaced with cards from the *demon*.

The first player to get through his *demon* shouts 'STOP!' Points are then allocated as follows: ten for finishing first; five for every time a player completes a set in the middle of the table by playing a King; and one for every other card in the middle. When the game recommences, whoever won the previous round adds an extra card to his *demon* by way of handicap.

Whoever collects the most points after say, ten rounds, is the winner.

7
GAMES
for practical jokers

There's always someone at every party who sets himself up to be the butt of a practical joke. And they usually fall into one of the following categories:

★ They are too drunk, overexcited, and run around madly, breaking things.
★ They have committed some pecadillo, such as making an improper suggestion to the Vicar's wife (or indeed to the Vicar himself) during a round of *Chinese Whispers*.
★ They have won all the prizes.
★ They have cheated unashamedly in every game.
★ They won't join in, even though you've played your way through Chapter 2.

Whatever the crime — and there are many more which could be added to the list — you can use it as an excuse to play one of the games in this Chapter.

That should teach them!

ARE YOU THERE MORIARTY?

Props: Two newspapers (broadsheets are best)

Preparation: Choose two players with tough skulls

There is a primitive pleasure to be had in watching two people beat each other's brains out with rolled copies of *The Times*. No more so than if they have worked their way through your supply of drink and female friends, and, in a state of Bacchic exuberance, threaten to cause serious damage to your house. A round of *Moriarty* will dispense of any surplus energy — and the pair might even knock each other out. You never know your luck.

Nigel and Henry (the game is considered a *scream* in county circles) lie flat on their tummies, each grasping the other's left wrist with his left hand, and a rolled newspaper with his right. Nigel calls out to Henry 'Are you there Moriarty?' to which, Henry replies, 'Yes' or 'Coo-ee!', before rolling to one side as Nigel attempts to beat his skull with the newspaper.

The game proceeds in this artless fashion, with players taking it in turns to smite and be smitten. The player who strikes the greatest number of direct blows is the winner. I have noticed that *The Sunday Times* has expanded to quite enormous proportions in recent months. You could successfully fix the game by arming your favourite with this, colour supplement and all.

PARACHUTE

Props: Two trays and a blindfold

Preparation: Buttonhole two strong types beforehand and explain what will be required of them when the game begins

This game will deflate the most bumptious of egos. It only works if you have a couple of willing musclemen in your midst.

Your Parachutist stands blindfolded on a tray — not of the dainty silver variety. You tell him that he will be raised high on the tray, and that when he feels his head touch the ceiling, he must jump.

The two musclemen now pick up the tray, and raise it waist high. They then drop slowly to a crouching position. The victim, his hands on their shoulders, will imagine that he is actually ascending as he feels them drop beneath him. He is in fact, now only a couple of inches from the ground. His face should reflect this, and if it doesn't, give the tray a wobble.

As the tray bearers sink, so another person — who will need to be tall — gently brings a second tray down to rest on the Parachutist's head. Thinking he has reached the ceiling, the Parachutist will prepare himself for an almighty leap and . . . well, the rest you can imagine.

PICTURE FRAME

Props: An empty picture frame

Preparation: Drape your unfortunate victim in some old sheets so that his clothes are not spoiled

This is akin to the cruel and ancient English custom of putting the village idiot in the stocks.

Find an empty picture frame and instruct your resident idiot (usually someone good natured and with a great sense of humour) to hold it up before his face. The rest of you now caper in front of him, leering, hurling insults (nothing too personal!) and pulling silly faces.

On no account must the idiot so much as blink. And if he either laughs (or cries) he must be subjected to a few well-aimed missiles — rotten tomatoes, soggy tea bags and the like. Great fun, if a little unkind on the carpet.

TRAINS

Props: None

Preparation: None — this is totally impromptu

It all starts off in an innocent-seeming way. One of you, who knows the game, leaps up from the dinner table and starts chuff-chuffing and toot-tooting around the table in a passable imitation of the 10.10 London to Brighton (circa 1920.)

As you complete your circle you pluck someone of the opposite sex from the table, tell them to link up behind you, and lead them chuffing and tooting out of the room. You shut the door.

Alone, you make as if to kiss the person. But just before your lips meet, you slap them instead. Hastily, you then explain that it's nothing personal, that it's part of the game, that it's their turn next, and *isn't this fun?*

All forgiven, the pair of you return, pick up someone else and take them outside. This time, you give the person you picked a kiss. They then turn to the new person who, with lips expectantly pursed, receives a slap. This process is repeated until everybody has received similar treatment.

The slapping may well hurt, but anyone who is picked in the early stages should count themselves lucky. Nothing is more painful than the ignominy of being the last player to be chosen. Such unfortunates may be found later in the evening conducting secret and solitary B.O./halitosis/personality tests in the bathroom.

THE DREAM GAME

Props: Vivid imaginations

Preparation: None

Men make the most satisfactory 'victims' in this game, which is a bawdy version of *Yes, No and Maybe*. If you have an ageing Romeo who has been pinching the ladies' bottoms, he'll do nicely — the more he fancies his chances the better.

Send Romeo out of the room, telling him that you are going to concoct a dream sequence tailor-made for him. When he returns, you tell him that he will have to ask everyone else questions and from their answers reconstruct the dream.

Once he is safely out of earshot, you let everyone else in on the secret: no dream is to be concocted, and Romeo is about to humiliate himself by revealing his secret fantasies. This is how it works:

Enter Romeo.

Romeo(lewdly): 'Is there a woman in my dream?'
A: 'But of course'
Romeo: 'Is she dressed . . . well . . . in her work clothes?'
B:'Oh, yes'.
Romeo: 'Sort of authoritarian?'
C:'Mmmm'
Romeo (with feigned casualness): 'She isn't a traffic warden, is she?'
D: 'How did you guess?!'

This is, of course, an abridged version of what might happen. But it should make the point. No dream has been decided on. A,B,C and co. merely agree with whatever Romeo suggests, and he hoists himself with his own petard.

NELSON'S EYE

Props: A ripe banana and a blindfold

Preparation: None to speak of

A nice trick to play on a lady — especially if she is squeamish.

Your victim is blindfolded and led over to another player, who has assumed the identity of Nelson.

One of you takes the victim's hand and guides it over the relevant parts of the Admiral's anatomy, saying as you do so: 'This is Nelson's arm . . .', 'This is Nelson's stump', 'This is Nelson's face', 'This is Nelson's sword', and so on . . .

Having built to a crescendo of tension, you say something like, 'As you know, Nelson lost an eye in battle (pause for effect) so this is Nelson's EYE SOCKET!' At this point you plunge your victim's finger deep into the pulp of an overripe banana. She, I can promise, will scream.

And loud.

WHO'S WHO

Props: A blindfold

Preparation: Tell everybody — bar the blindfolded player —
how the game proceeds

Once more, your unhappy victim is blindfolded and, on this
occasion, let loose to wander about a room with the rest of
you. His job is to feel the other players and to guess who it is
he is pawing.

It can get embarrassing.

At a given moment you all begin to creep out of the room,
leaving the victim to stagger about blindly until he works out
the trick, or to grasp hold of a chair leg, a bannister or a lamp
stand, and announce with triumph and glee that he has got
hold of Uncle Percy's wooden leg.

RUSSIAN OMELETTE

Props: An egg per player

Preparation: Hard boil all but one of the eggs

The players gather around the table, mock-serious expressions on their faces. An egg for each player is placed in the middle of the table, all hard-boiled...save one. Everyone takes it in turn to pick up one of the eggs and crack it hard against his skull. Relief if it's a ten-minuter. A mess if it isn't.

Of course, none of this is much fun if your first player picks the dud egg — it rather kills off the tension, which can be quite considerable. So you can always enliven the game by deciding beforehand who deserves to be punished, placing them last and secretly telling all the other players not to pick the speckled/brown or otherwise identifiable egg.

Russian Omelette requires no skill whatsoever, and the more dulled your sensations, the better.

BANANA GAME

Props: Three bananas and a blindfold

Preparation: Take two of your banana-eaters to one side before the game begins, and explain to them how you will trick the third player

> 'Who likes banana?'
> 'Me.'
> 'Me.'
> 'Me'.

Greedy young men and show-offs always volunteer, and you'll have trouble paring the flurry of offers down to three. But you must.

When you've made your choice, tell the players that the game is a race, and that the winner is whoever can eat his banana the fastest − blindfolded.

What actually happens is that only one player is blindfolded and given a banana. At the word 'Go!' he will frantically cram his banana into his mouth and chomp at high speed, believing that the other players are doing likewise. You sustain this belief with cries of 'Come on Tom!', 'Go for it Dick!' and 'Beat them Harry!'

When the banana is consumed, you all cheer, and your victim emerges from his blindfold triumphant, only to realise he has been duped.

YES, NO AND MAYBE

Props: None

Preparation: None

One player is selected and sent from the room, blithely unaware of the fact that he is to be made an utter fool of (at least, that's the idea). Before he leaves, you tell him that the rest of you are going to compose a narrative which he must unravel by questions which can only be answered with a 'Yes', a 'No' or a 'Maybe'.

Once the door is closed behind him, you inform the remaining players that no such thing is to happen. Instead, you explain that the last word of each of the first player's questions will determine the answer — 'Yes' if the last word ends in a consonant, 'No' if it ends in a vowel, and 'Maybe' if it ends with the letter 'Y'.

The first player now returns, and questions each of you in turn.

'Is the story set in Paraguay?'
'Maybe.'
(Baffled already) 'Does it involve me?'
'No. '
'Does it involve anyone I know?'
'Yes.'
'My mother?'
'Yes.'

This can go on for literally hours, with the first player becoming more red-faced and confused by the minute. 20 minutes is probably a wise time limit to set. If your victim hasn't cottoned on by this stage, he will have earned himself the leading role in a round of *Picture Frame* (see page 96)

THE BLANKET GAME

Props: A blanket

Preparation: Give some careful thought about who you intend sending under the blanket. . .

A titillating game which which has been known to cause serious marital rifts — so watch out.

A man and a woman who are unfamiliar with the game (and preferably with each other) lie on the floor and are covered with the blanket. The other players gather round them and tell them that they are both wearing something and that they are both to remove it. Pause, snigger, and what is likely to be passed out from under the blanket is a pair of shoes — one masculine, one feminine. 'I'm afraid that's not what we had in mind, 'you say. Pause, more sniggering, and out come two more shoes, or two rings or two shirts.

Clearly this game can get a little racy, and just how far you want to take it will depend upon your morals, the morals of the people under the blanket and how much you have all had to drink. The point, however, is that at a given moment you let the pair into the secret, and tell them that what you have been after all along is the blanket. So saying, you whip it off and leave the pair lying there feeling quite silly, and perhaps a little cold.

HOW DO YOU DO?

Props: Two blindfolds

Preparation: None

All of you — save two players (preferably one of either sex) — form two lines, facing one another about two metres apart. Blindfolded, the pair must walk towards each other from either end of the two lines. When they meet, they must shake hands and say 'How do you do?' Until they meet, they must not call out to each other.

 You cannot direct them or otherwise help them unless they bypass each other altogether and therefore need to be turned around and sent back. The spectacle of the pair staggering up and down the lines, arms outstretched, is highly entertaining, although your victims, after the first twenty minutes or so, may be forgiven if they begin to think otherwise.

8
GAMES
for goons

There comes a point during most parties when good sense goes out of the window. The sober become quite giddy, a general frivolity holds sway and almost anything will reduce the lot of you to bouts of agonising, hysterical giggling.

Well into the party mood by now, you have dealt with your shyness and inhibitions, and are ready to play any game that's suggested — so long as the rules aren't intellectually too demanding. (*Pinochle* is therefore quite out of the question.)

This is where the really silly games come into their own. Read on . . . if you are still able.

FEED THE BABY

Props: Baby bottles filled with milk, champagne or some other liquid (preferably potable); bibs; bootees and bonnets (optional)

Preparation: Decide before you begin who is to be paired off with whom

This game was probably invented by some sick-minded individual with an original line in fantasies. That could be why it's such a hoot.

First of all you must divide the players into couples, the more unlikely the better. The woman in each pair is then given a bib and a bottle and sent to sit at the far end of the room.

At the word 'Go!', each man races to his partner and sits on her lap. She ties the bib around his neck, and feeds him from the bottle. Once the bottle is emptied, the woman wipes her 'baby's' mouth, removes his bib, and the pair race to the other end of the room. The first couple to get there wins.

You can, of course, dress the babies up in all sorts of additional gear. I have found that socks are good substitute bootees, while boxer shorts worn on the head make very attractive bonnets.

THE CHOCOLATE GAME

Props: A bar of chocolate, a knife, a fork, a blindfold and some music

Preparation: Put the chocolate in the freezer for several hours before the game begins

Some poor fool is elected to take charge of the music. If you have an aged relative with you, this could be a good job for them.

The rest of you sit in a circle on the floor, placing a frozen bar of chocolate and a knife and fork in the middle of the circle. One of you is designated the first player.

On goes the music, and when it stops the first player leaps into the middle of the circle, dons the blindfold, and tries to eat the frozen chocolate with the knife and fork. As soon as the music starts again, he downs his tools, removes the blindfold, and dives back to his place in the circle. When the music stops once more, the player to his left charges into the middle of the circle, puts on the blindfold and attacks the chocolate.

And so the game continues, with players darting in and out of the circle, each desperate to get a crumb of chocolate into his mouth before the music starts up again. If you have no music, or if nobody wants to be left controlling it, you can take turns to thow a dice — whenever a six is thrown, the next player tackles the chocolate bar.

The game finishes when all the chocolate is eaten.

EGYPTIAN MUMMIES

Props: Loo paper

Preparation: Pay a visit to Egypt and take a look at a few Pharaohs

In this game, men are entirely at the mercy of women. Both sexes are therefore in their element.

Divide the players into mixed pairs, and give each pair a roll of soft loo paper. At the word 'Go!', the women swaddle their partners from top to toe in the paper, making sure they cover every inch of the body (save the nose — you don't want your male guests to expire!).

It's good to set a time limit of two or three minutes, and at the end of this, each mummy hops around the room in a sort of beauty pageant.

The best-wrapped mummy wins a prize.

CHICKEN FEED

Props: An old pack of cards

Preparation: Exercise your forefinger

This is a mindless game which requires only a sharp eye and a strong finger. The aim is to spot, and lay claim to, more playing cards than anybody else. This is how it's done.

One of you is elected Umpire. The rest of you gather in a circle on the floor. The Umpire spreads out a pack of cards face up in the middle of the circle, and then calls out a card name — say, the Jack of Hearts. You all scan the floor for the card, and whoever spots it, stabs the card with his forefinger, and drags it back to where he is sitting. Several players may, of course, stab at the same time, at which point it becomes a question of whose finger is the stronger. Alternatively, the card may tear in half, thirds, quarters or more.

The game goes on like this, with new cards being called and claimed by the players. The winner is whoever has the most (whole) cards at the end, and he wins a prize.

CARD SCRAMBLE

Props: An old pack of playing cards cut in half

Preparation: None (although rugby players have a real advantage)

This is the sort of game that you play at the end of a long evening, when you've worked your way through all the other, more sensible, games. It's not unlike *Chicken Feed*.

The pack of cards, cut in unequal portions, is thrown in a random heap on the floor. Everyone drops to their knees and scrabbles wildly for both halves of as many cards as possible. The game can get quite violent as players compete for possession of bits of card, and some knuckle-bashing and eye-gouging might ensue. This is quite normal, so don't be alarmed.

At the end of the battle, whoever has taken possession of the highest number of matching halves is the winner.

It goes without saying that it is highly unethical to pocket, sit upon, eat or otherwise secrete bits of card in order to flummox other players. And watch out for women wearing full-skirted frocks — they tend to hoard cards underneath them, and should be made to pay a forfeit if caught doing so.

BOTTOMS

Props: None

Preparation: None

This is one of those unsophisticated games best kept for the end of the evening, when everyone has the giggles, and when lavatory humour has ceased to shock.

One player asks the other players questions: 'What's your favourite food?', 'How do you keep your figure?', 'What are you reading at University?'

Whatever the question, and whoever it's addressed to, the answer must always be the same: 'Bottoms' And it must be delivered with a straight face. Any player who sniggers or even smirks is instantly out.

It is possible that the word 'Bottoms' doesn't make you laugh, and that you have your own funny word. Fine. I leave the suggestions to you.

GHOSTS

Props: A sheet

Preparation: Psyche yourselves up with one of the murder games — that way you might even find this harmless pursuit frightening.

Another undemanding pastime.

Players are divided into two teams. One team leaves the room, taking with it the sheet. The second team sits down and waits to be amused. Members of the first team now appear at the door, one at a time, draped in the sheet and wailing in a phantasmagoric fashion. Those seated in the room have to guess the identity of each ghost as it appears.

The two teams then swop places. The team which makes the highest number of correct guesses wins.

SQUEAK PIGGY SQUEAK

Props: A blindfold

Preparation: None — although some people might need to rehearse their squeaking

All the players — save one — sit in a circle on the floor. The remaining player is blindfolded, turned around a few times, and left standing in the middle of the circle.

At random he chooses a lap of one of the seated players and sits on it, calling out as he does. 'Squeak piggy squeak!' The owner of the lap squeaks and squeals like a piglet, and if the blindfolded player can identify the person he's sitting on, the pair swop places.

The game then proceeds in the same way until it ceases to amuse or someone is flattened by a fatty.

DEAD PAN

Props: None

Preparation: Practise keeping a straight face

Dead Pan requires self-control, which is why it can only be played when most of you have lost yours.

Everyone sits around a table, or in a circle on the floor and assumes a deadly earnest expression. One player, who has been designated Leader, prods the player sitting on his left, who then prods the player on *his* left. The prod is passed round the circle until it comes back to the Leader. He then pinches, tickles or otherwise molests his neighbour and this is passed round the circle.

For the next round, the Leader might choose to kiss his neighbour or insult him — anything goes. The point is that, all the while, the rest of the players must keep straight faces. At the slightest hint of a smile the Leader will eliminate you.

The winner is the last player to remain dead pan.

ACTIONS

Props: None

Preparation: Nothing will prepare you for this if you just don't have a sense of rhythm and natural coordination.

An excellent game to play if people are starting to flag. This will liven them up.

You all stand in a wide circle. The first player starts the game off by performing an action — say tapping the top of his head. The player on his left copies the action and follows it with one of his own — jumping in the air, for instance. Player number three now has to tap his head, jump in the air and perform a third action — blowing a raspberry perhaps. The next player taps his head, jumps in the air, blows a raspberry and clicks his fingers. And so it continues.

If you miss an action, or perform the actions in the wrong order, or if you simply collapse in a heap on the floor, you're out .

The winner is whoever survives this marathon to the bitter end.

THE GOLF BALL RACE

Props: Two golf balls, two buckets and two soft chairs

Preparation: Do some of those buttock-building exercises — walking up and down the bathroom on your bottom, etc

Put one of the golf balls on each of the chairs, place the chairs at one end of the room, the buckets at the other, and divide your players into two teams. Each of the teams lines up behind a chair

At the word 'Go!'the first player in each team runs round to the front of his chair and picks up the golf ball between his buttocks — no hands allowed. He then waddles as best he can, and as fast as he can, down to his bucket and, crouching over it, drops the golf ball in. If all this is accomplished without a hitch, he then picks up the golf ball (in his hand, this time), runs back to the front of the chair and the next player repeats the whole performance. And a performance it generally is!

If the player's posterior loses its grip and the ball escapes, then the player must pick it up (in his hand), carry it back to the chair and start his lap from the beginning.

Some people favour ping pong balls, but I have found that they are easily mashed between over-zealous buttocks, and are therefore not much good. Eggs are just plain messy.

THE COMMUTER GAME

Props: A jumbled newspaper and a chair per player

Preparation: A lifetime of grim early-morning train journeys

You probably won't want more than about eight players for this game. Anybody who is unfortunate enough to commute by train will have to be among the eight. The rest of you are spectators.

Arrange the chairs so that they are in a closely-packed line, and give each of the players a newspaper with all its pages jumbled up, and out of order. At the word 'GO!' the players wedge themselves into the chairs, and attempt to reorganize their newspapers — not the easiest of tasks when performed under conditions reminiscent of the 07.49 East Croydon to London Bridge.

Whoever successfully overcomes the various handicaps (principally lack of elbow room) and sorts out his paper first is the winner.

FEEDING THE BRUTE

Props: A tube of Smarties and blindfolds for all the women

Preparation: None

Players form pairs and line up in two rows facing one another, women in one line, men in the other. All the women are blindfolded and given a Smartie. The women then have to find their partners and feed them the Smarties. The men cannot move their heads, call out 'I'm over here you clot!', or otherwise assist their partner. They must simply stand with their mouths open wide like baby cuckoos, hoping that their partner doesn't extract one of their eyes with a fingernail.

   The chances are that few of the feeders will find the right mouth and successfully dispose of their Smartie. If, however, the game proves too easy, you could try playing it again — this time with jelly or custard and a spoon.

THE WIND AND THE LEAVES

Props: A large room with a door that leads out of the house

Preparation: Not much . . .

One for when you want to get rid of everyone, but aren't quite sure how to achieve this tactfully.

You tell your guests that you are the Wind, and that they are all Leaves. You then explain that each corner of the room is one of the four cardinal points (North, South, East, West), and that each time that you, the Wind, change direction, they, the Leaves, must all rush to the appropriate corner.

The Leaves huddle together in the middle of the room, and when you call out 'North!' the Leaves run to that corner. If you call out 'South', so they run to that corner. If you call out 'Tempest!' everyone charges around madly in all directions until another command is issued.

When you've decided enough's enough you call out 'East!' (or whichever corner the door is in), and then open the door. In their enthusiasm, the Leaves will all run outside. You then slam the door and go upstairs to bed.